Logic and Critical Thinking

WRITTEN BY
MARGARET THOMAS

ILLUSTRATED BY
MARTY BUCELLA

COVER BY
JEFF VAN KANEGAN

Publisher
Instructional Fair • TS Denison
Grand Rapids, MI 49544

Instructional Fair • TS Denison grants the individual purchaser permission to reproduce patterns and student activity materials in this book for noncommercial individual or classroom use only. Reproduction for an entire school or school system is strictly prohibited. No other part of this publication may be reproduced in whole or in part. No part of this publication may be reproduced for storage in a retrieval system, or transmitted in any form or by any means, electronic, mechanical, recording, or otherwise, without the prior written permission of the publisher. For information regarding permission, write to Instructional Fair • TS Denison, P.O. Box 1650, Grand Rapids, MI 49501.

ISBN: 0-7424-0086-7
Logic and Critical Thinking
Copyright © 2001 Instructional Fair • TS Denison
a Division of Instructional Fair Group, Inc.
3195 Wilson Dr. NW
Grand Rapids, Michigan 49544

All Rights Reserved • Printed in the USA

How to Use This Book

The Mathematical Mind series consists of six books, *Logic and Critical Thinking; Computation and Number Sense; Ratio, Proportion, and Percent; Geometry; Pre-Algebra;* and *Probability and Statistics.* The books contain mathematics information and activities intended for use at the middle-grade level. The contents complement the math concepts presented in the classroom.

Several activities are self-checking with answers that complete a puzzle or a riddle. Most of the activities are one page in length. The activities may be used by teachers in the classroom or by individual students to review, reinforce, and extend middle-grade mathematics. Information from other disciplines is included to motivate students. Definitions, examples, and brief explanations are included, making the activities student-oriented. The activity sheets are intended to be used by teachers as blackline copymasters. The books could be used by individuals as consumable workbooks. An answer key is provided in each book.

Logic and Critical Thinking includes activities which review and reinforce problem-solving strategies and spatial visualization. The strategies include using tables, drawing diagrams, graph analysis, guess and check, changing point of view, working backwards, patterns and sequences, understanding connections, number sense, and checking solutions. Logic tables and Venn diagrams are used to organize data in order to draw conclusions and solve problems. Both discrete and continuous graphs are included to demonstrate relationships between variables. Codes, sequences, and patterns are analyzed by using number sense and computation rules. Spatial visualization activities use drawings of cubes, base plans, and isometric views. Several activities include information concerning mountain peaks, tea consumption, presidents, and states. The formats include free response questions, matching activities, multiple choice problems, mazes, and puzzles.

Table of Contents

"X" It Out! 5
Tea for Two! 6
"Climb Every Mountain" 7
A Class Act 8
Sports Lunch 9
Bench Warmers 10
Table Talk 11
How Many Are There? 12
Show Me the Graph 13
A Graph Is Worth a Thousand Words 14
Balancing Act 15
Pet Shop 16
Get Organized 17
I Am Unique 18
It's Like 19
Body Parts 20
Initial Equations 21
Everyone's a Critic 22
On Second Thought 23
Animal Pathways 24
Working Backwards 25
Begin at the End 26
Arrow Paths 27
Next, Please! 28
Pattern Problems 29
Code Math 30
Gizmos, Whatsits, and Whatchamacallits 31
Common Features 32
Cube It! 33
Face It! 34
From All Angles 35
Covering the Bases 36
Reading Rebuses 37
Reading Rebuses (con't.) 38
Word Pictures 39
Cheaper by the Dozen 40
Broken Magic 41
Bingo 42
Line Up 43
Digit Math 44
Answer Key 45

Name_____

"X" It Out

Allen, Bob, Carl, David, and Earl live in Albany, Baltimore, Chicago, Denver, and Erie.

CLUES
1. No one lives in a city starting with the same letter as his name.
2. Allen always has a layover in Chicago when he flies west to visit Earl.
3. Carl enjoys his view of the lake.
4. Since David is a state official, he lives in a capital city.

Use the clues and table. Use Xs to eliminate possibilities. As you figure out each clue, cross out the other boxes in that row and column.

	Albany	Baltimore	Chicago	Denver	Erie
Allen	X				
Bob		X			
Carl			X		
David				X	
Earl					X

HINTS

Clue #1 states that Allen does not live in Albany, Bob does not live in Baltimore, Carl does not live in Chicago, David does not live in Denver, and Earl does not live in Erie. Xs have been placed in the corresponding cells of the table. Use the other clues (not necessarily in order) to eliminate other possibilities.

RESULTS
1. Allen lives in _____.
2. Bob lives in _____.
3. Carl lives in _____.
4. David lives in _____.
5. Earl lives in _____.

TEA FOR TWO!

Name_____

Tea is a popular drink around the world. The top six tea-consuming countries in alphabetical order are Australia, Great Britain, Ireland, New Zealand, Sri Lanka, and Turkey. The approximate consumption rates (cups per person per year) in numerical order are 635, 640, 650, 890, 1300, and 1355.

CLUES
1. Australians drink less than their neighbor New Zealanders but more than the people of Sri Lanka.
2. It should be no surprise that the British consume the most tea.
3. The Irish drink twice as much as Turks.

Use the clues and table. Use Xs to eliminate possibilities. As you figure out each match (country and cups), X-out the other boxes in that row and column.

Countries	635	640	650	890	1300	1355
Australia						
Great Britain						
Ireland						
New Zealand						
Sri Lanka						
Turkey						

RESULTS
1. Australia _____
2. Great Britain _____
3. Ireland _____
4. New Zealand _____
5. Sri Lanka _____
6. Turkey _____

© Instructional Fair • TS Denison   6   IF2906 Logic and Critical Thinking

"Climb Every Mountain"

The highest peak on each continent: Aconcagua (South America), Cook (Australia), Elbrus (Europe), Everest (Asia), Kilimanjaro (Africa), McKinley (North America), and Vinson Massif (Antarctica) were first ascended in the years 1874, 1889, 1894, 1897, 1913, 1953, and 1966 (not in order).

CLUES:
1. The South American peak was ascended before the North American peak but after Cook was scaled.
2. Forty years after McKinley was ascended, Hillary ascended Everest.
3. It is not surprising that the Antarctica peak was the most recent, more than 90 years after Gardiner ascended Elbrus, and more than 75 years after Meyer and Purtscgheller ascended Kilimanjaro.

Use the clues and table. Use Xs to eliminate possibilities. As you figure out each match (peak and year), X-out the boxes in that row and column.

Peaks	1874	1889	1894	1897	1913	1953	1966
Aconcagua							
Cook							
Elbrus							
Everest							
Kilimanjaro							
McKinley							
Vinson Massif							

RESULTS
1. Aconcagua (South America) _____
2. Cook (Australia) _____
3. Elbrus (Europe) _____
4. Everest (Asia) _____
5. Kilimanjaro (Africa) _____
6. McKinley (North America) _____
7. Vinson Massif (Antarctica) _____

© Instructional Fair • TS Denison   IF2906 *Logic and Critical Thinking*

Name_____

A Class Act

Ali, Brianna, and Calli are each taking two classes from the following list: art, biology, chemistry, engineering, English, and law. No two students are in the same class. Who is taking which courses?

CLUES
1. Calli met Brianna and the art student at the library.
2. Brianna tutors the English student.
3. The chemistry and English students had lunch with Ali.
4. The biology student rooms with the chemistry student.
5. The art student and the engineering student are sisters.
6. The biology student let the art student decorate her apartment.

	Art	Biology	Chemistry	Engineering	English	Law
Ali	O					
Brianna	X					
Calli	X					

HINTS
The table shows the information from Clue 1. The other spaces in the "Ali row" cannot be X-ed out yet because Ali is taking a second class. Remember since Ali is taking art, every clue referring to the art student also refers to Ali. Use the other clues to complete the table.

RESULTS
1. Ali is enrolled in _____ and _____.

2. Brianna is enrolled in _____ and _____.

3. Calli is enrolled in _____ and _____.

Sports Lunch

Zach, Bob, Sam, and Tony each play a different sport. At lunch they sat around a square table.

1. The baseball player sat on Bob's left.

2. Zach and Sam sat across from each other.

3. The football player sat across from Tony.

4. Zach sat to the right of the basketball player.

   Who plays hockey? _____

Use the illustration and the table to match the player with his sport.

	Zach	Bob	Sam	Tony
Baseball				
Basketball				
Football				
Hockey				

Name_____

BENCH WARMERS

Use the clues to place the people on each bench.

1. Pat, Raul, Steve, and Tom are sitting on a bench.
   - Tom is sitting left of Pat and Raul.
   - Steve is sitting to the right of Raul.
   - Raul is not sitting next to Tom.

   Label the boys sitting on the bench.

2. A string quartet is sitting on a bench. The members are Anna, Betty, Carol, and Dee.
   - Carol is between the violinist and the cellist.
   - The cellist is sitting at one end of the bench.
   - Dee, the bass player, is sitting at the other end.
   - Anna sits between Dee and Carol.
   - Betty is sitting left of Carol, the viola player.

   Label the girls sitting on the bench.

   What does Anna play? _____

   What does Betty play? _____

3. Five members of the Thomas family, Bob, Margie, Jenny, Katie, and Robert are sitting on a bench.
   - The kids are separated by the parents, Bob and Margie.
   - Katie and Jenny are sitting to the right of their dad.
   - Jenny is sitting left of her mom.

   Label the family members.
   Who is sitting in the middle? _____

© Instructional Fair • TS Denison   10   IF2906 Logic and Critical Thinking

Name_____

TABLE TALK

Draw a diagram to help solve each problem.

1. Fourteen people are sitting equally spaced around a circular table. If the seats are numbered 1 through 14, who is sitting across from 5? _____

2. Ten square tables, each seating four people, are pushed together to form one long rectangular table. How many people can be seated? _____

3. Eight square tables, each seating four people, are pushed together into a U-shape. Only one person can sit at each "inside corner." How many people can be seated? _____

4a. There are 24 square tables. How many large rectangular tables can be made using all 24 tables? _____

4b. Give the dimensions of each table.
_____

4c. How many people can be seated at each table? _____

5. Five people attend a dinner party. If every person shakes hands with all other people at the party, how many handshakes will there be?
_____

© Instructional Fair • TS Denison IF2906 Logic and Critical Thinking

Name_____

How Many Are There?

For each situation, complete the given Venn diagram to answer the question.

1. Terry has six blue shirts, five green shirts, and three striped shirts. If two of the blue shirts are striped, how many shirts are there? _____

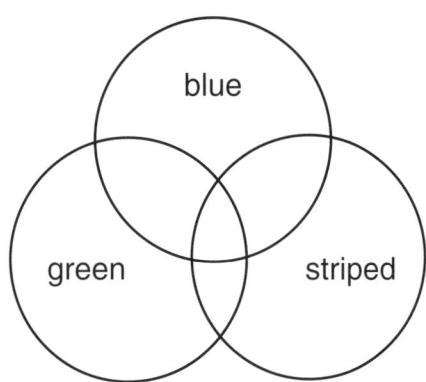

2. Joni likes animals and riddles. When asked how many pets she had, she offered the following riddle: Five of my pets have tails. Six of my pets have hair. Three have tails and hair. How many pets do I have? _____

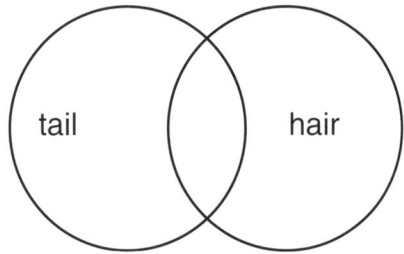

3. Eli surveyed his classmates as to their preferences for vegetables. Twelve like corn, ten like green beans, fifteen like peas, and three do not like any of the choices. Eight of the students who like peas also like green beans, and five of the students like all three vegetables. How many students are there? _____

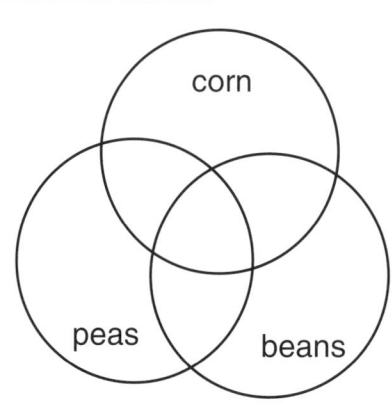

4. In Mr. Martin's class every student belongs to at least one science club. Ten joined the ecology club. Fifteen participated in Science Olympiad. Nine started a recycling group. If three students belong to all three clubs, and six belong to both the ecology and the recycling group, how many students are there? _____

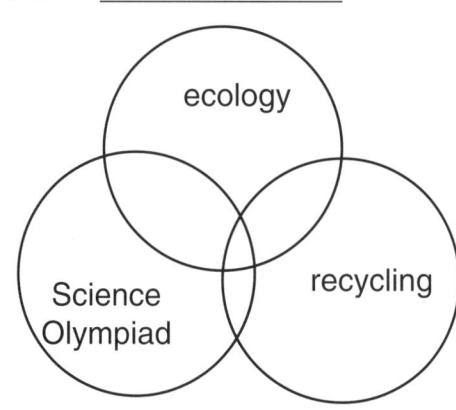

© Instructional Fair • TS Denison   IF2906 *Logic and Critical Thinking*

Name_____

SHOW ME THE GRAPH

Which of the following graphs most likely shows . . .

A. relationship between centimeters and inches?
B. pairs of possible positive integer factors of 24?
C. cost of postage compared to weight?
D. resale value of a car based on its age?
E. growth of virus over time?
F. time awake versus time asleep?

1. _____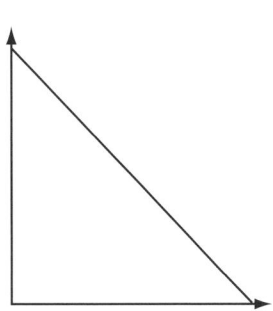

4. _____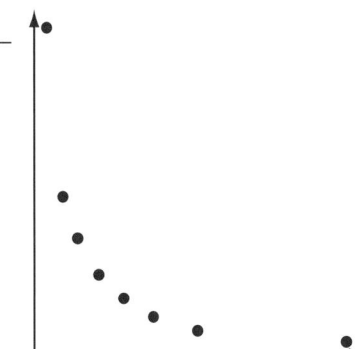

2. _____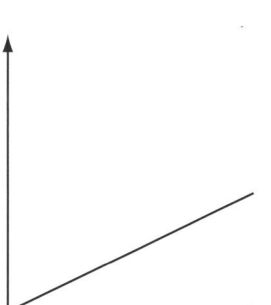

5. _____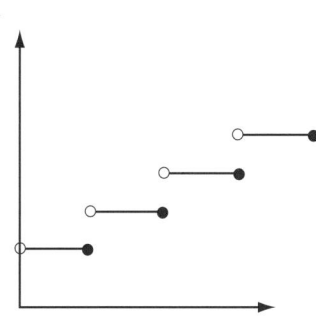

3. _____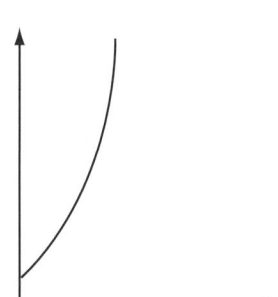

6. _____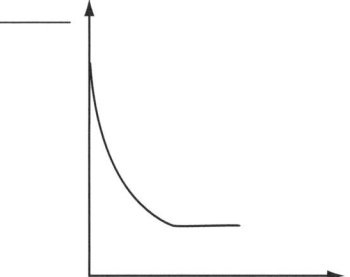

A Graph Is Worth a Thousand Words

1. Robert traveled by car from his house to a store. The graph represents his trip. Match the intervals with what might have happened.

   A. ____   1. Drives on a neighborhood street
   B. ____   2. Stops at a one-minute stop light
   C. ____   3. Drives on a freeway
   D. ____   4. Drives into a parking spot
   E. ____   5. Stops in parking spot
   F. ____   6. Stops briefly at a stop sign

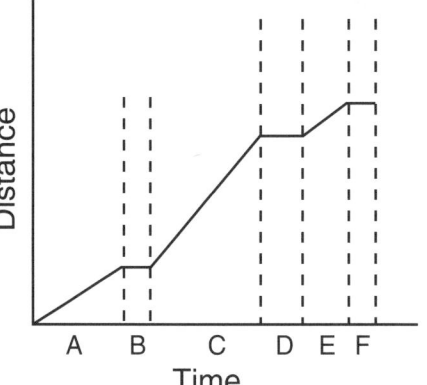

2. The graph pertains to a boy, his dog, and a tub of water. Explain what might have happened during each interval.

   A. _____
   B. _____
   C. _____
   D. _____
   E. _____
   F. _____
   G. _____

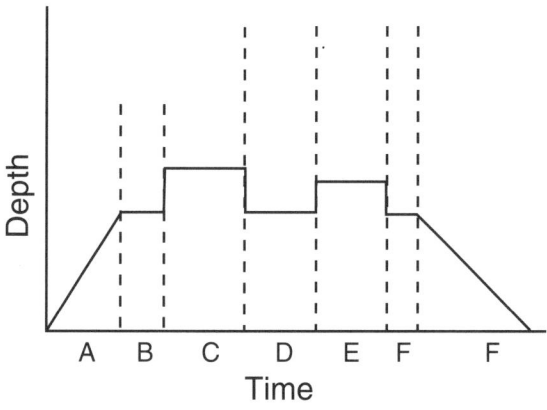

3. What carnival ride might be associated with this graph of distance above the ground versus time?

   _____

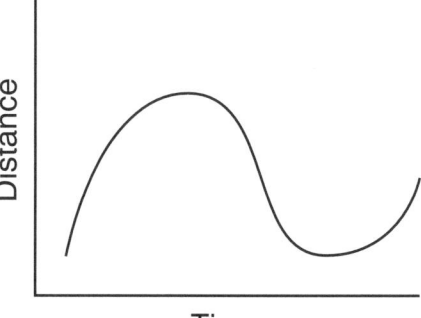

Balancing Act

Name_____

Use balances A and B to determine the missing quantity on balance C. Hint: First step for problem 1—Replace the two △s on balance A with the equivalent three ○s from balance B.

1.
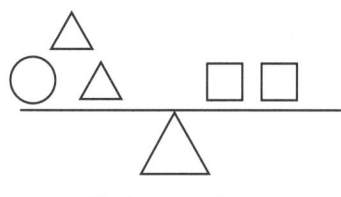 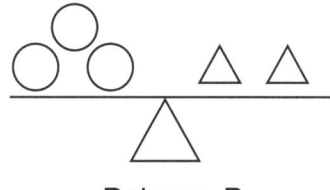 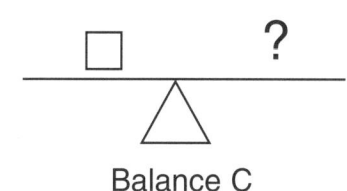

Balance A   Balance B   Balance C

2.
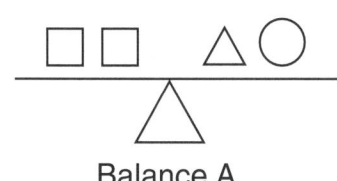 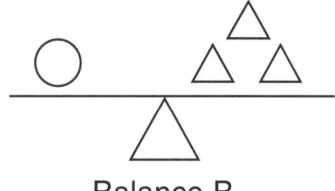 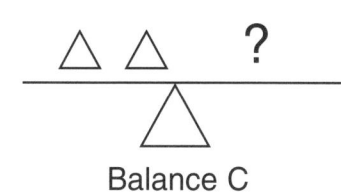

Balance A   Balance B   Balance C

3.
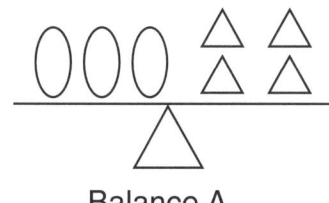  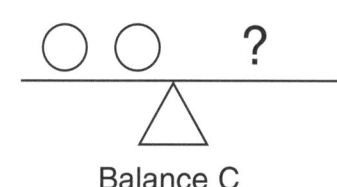

Balance A   Balance B   Balance C

4.
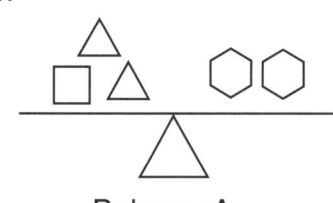 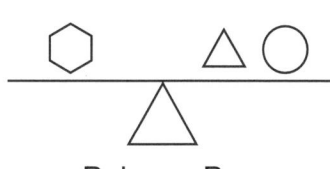 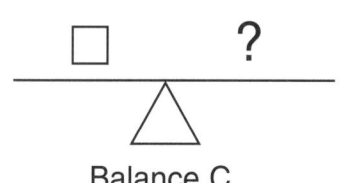

Balance A   Balance B   Balance C

© Instructional Fair • TS Denison   IF2906 *Logic and Critical Thinking*

PET SHOP

Name _____

One way to solve these problems is to "guess and check." Use a table to organize your guesses. If necessary, extend the tables on another sheet of paper.

1. Sally's Shoppe specializes in sparrows and spaniels. When asked how many of each animal she had, she responded, "There are 51 heads and 180 legs." How many of each animal does Sally have? Sparrows _____ Spaniels _____

Sparrows	Legs	Spaniels	Legs	Total Heads	Total Legs	Check?
40	80	11	44	51	124	no

2. Sally's sister Suzi bought supplies for the shop. She bought leashes for $10 each, chew toys for $3 each, and seed packets for $.50 each. If she paid $100 for 100 items, how many of each did she purchase?

Leashes _____   Chew toys _____   Seed Packets _____

Leashes	Cost	Chew Toys	Cost	Seed Packets	Cost	Total #	Total $	Check?
4	$40	16	$48	80	$40	100	$128	no

© Instructional Fair • TS Denison   IF2906 Logic and Critical Thinking

Name_____

GET ORGANIZED

Use a table to organize your "guesses." There may be more than one solution. If needed, extend the table on another sheet.

1. Find the dimensions of rectangles whose sides are whole numbers and numerically the units of perimeter equal the units of area.

L	W	Perimeter	Area	Check
1	1	4	2	no
2	1	6	2	no
2	2			

2. Mandy used 31 legs to make 4-legged benches and 3-legged stools. How many of each did she make?

Benches(4)	Stools(3)	Legs	Check
2	9	35	no
2	8	32	no

3. Using a dartboard like this, I scored exactly 100 points. How many darts did I throw and where did they land?

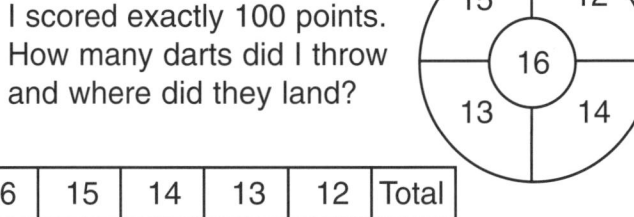

16	15	14	13	12	Total
5			1	1	105
4				3	100*

4. The Happy Hotel has blissful bedbugs. In each single bed there are 7 bedbugs, and in each double bed there are 13 bedbugs. If 106 bedbugs are at the hotel how many of each size of bed are there?

Single(7)	Double(13)	Total	Check

5. Jonathon paid $10.00 for some $.33 and $.20 stamps. How many of each did he buy?

$.33	$.20	Total	Check

6. Kerry counted 9 cycle riders and 25 wheels go past her house. How many bicycles and how many tricycles passed her house?

Bicycles	Tricycles	Wheels

I Am Unique

Each number given below is unique in at least one way compared to the other numbers. State at least one property of each number that makes it unique. Be creative.

Ex. Two is the only even prime number.

2

75

0.8

$12\frac{1}{2}$

1

17

-142

$\sqrt{3}$

$0.8\overline{6}$

$-\frac{1}{5}$

49

6.7

0

27

1,000

2/3

75%

279

3

250%

It's Like

Name_____

Give another example of what each person likes and dislikes. Then describe what each person likes.

1. Jake likes spaghetti, but not pasta.
   Jake likes jelly, but not jam.
   Jake likes pepper, but not salt.
   Jake likes cookies, but not cakes.
   Jake likes _____,
   but not _____
   because Jake likes _____
   _____.

2. Terry likes globes, but not maps.
   Terry likes oranges, but not bananas.
   Terry likes baseballs, but not footballs.
   Terry likes marbles, but not jacks.
   Terry likes _____,
   but not _____
   because Terry likes _____
   _____.

3. Sharon likes A, but not B.
   Sharon likes W, but not Q.
   Sharon likes V, but not N.
   Sharon likes Y, but not Z.
   Sharon likes _____,
   but not _____
   because Sharon likes _____
   _____.

4. Mac likes B, but not A.
   Mac likes H, but not R.
   Mac likes X, but not Y.
   Mac likes D, but not P.
   Mac likes _____,
   but not _____
   because Mac likes _____
   _____.

5. Neil likes 3, but not 4.
   Neil likes 5, but not 6.
   Neil likes 7, but not 8.
   Neil likes 9, but not 10.
   Neil likes _____,
   but not _____
   because Neil likes _____
   _____.

6. Nicole likes 2, but not 4.
   Nicole likes 3, but not 6.
   Nicole likes 5, but not 15.
   Nicole likes 7, but not 10.
   Nicole likes _____,
   but not _____
   because Nicole likes _____
   _____.

7. Judy likes 25, but not 30.
   Judy likes 15, but not 14.
   Judy likes 45, but not 70.
   Judy likes 65, but not 61.
   Judy likes _____,
   but not _____
   because Judy likes _____
   _____.

Body Parts

Give the part of the body that *sounds* the same as the item defined below.

1. Part of a yard
2. A student
3. A sailor's positive response
4. Used to measure the height of a horse
5. Part of a tree
6. Part of a comb
7. Tropical tree
8. Half of a diameter
9. Used to connect boards
10. Church musical instrument
11. Holland bulbs
12. Last slice of bread
13. A type of bean
14. A flower
15. Part of a shoe
16. Another part of a shoe
17. Type of rabbit
18. A box for treasure
19. A baby cow
20. Section that ends a book

1. <u>foot</u>
2. _____
3. _____
4. _____
5. _____
6. _____
7. _____
8. _____
9. _____
10. _____
11. _____
12. _____
13. _____
14. _____
15. _____
16. _____
17. _____
18. _____
19. _____
20. _____

INITIAL EQUATIONS

Each statement contains the initials of words that will make the equation true.

Example: 32 = D. F. at which W. F. becomes 32 = Degrees Fahrenheit at which Water Freezes

1. 24 = H. in a D.
2. 365 = D. in a Y. except L. Y.
3. 12 = I. in a F.
4. 30 = D. H. S. A. J. and N.
5. 88 = P. K.
6. 100 = C. in a D.
7. 9 = P. in the S. S.
8. 26 = L. of the A.
9. 90 = D. in a R. A.
10. 4 = Q. in a G.
11. 13 = S. on the A. F.
12. 16 = O. in a P.
13. 1,000 = M. in a K.
14. 9 = I. in a B. G.
15. 0 = D. C. at which W. F.
16. 12 = M. in a Y.
17. 52 = C. in a D.
18. 60 = S. in a M.
19. 2,000 = P. in a T.
20. 360 = D. in a C.

100 = P. in a D.

Name _____

Everyone's a Critic

Be a "critical problem solver" as you try to solve the following problems. The problems may not be as difficult as they intially appear. "Step back" and look at the problem from a different point of view. There may be unnecessary information.

1. A water lily doubles itself each day. From the time it was placed in a pond until the surface of the pond (600 sq ft) was completely covered took 30 days. How long did it take for the pond to be half-covered? _____

2. Two truckers drove from Dayton to Toledo and back. The first trucker drove to Toledo at 50 mph and returned to Dayton at 60 mph. The second trucker drove to Toledo and back at 55 mph. If the round trip is 300 miles, which driver took longer to make the round trip? _____

3. A phonograph record had a total diameter of 12 inches. The recording left an outer margin of 1 inch. The diameter of an unused center was 4 inches. There are an average of 90 grooves per inch. How far does a needle travel when the record is played? _____

4. A test track for new cars is one mile around. For the first lap, the driver averages 30 mph. How fast does the car have to travel a second lap to average 60 mph for the two laps? _____

5. Mary noticed that it takes 6 seconds for the town clock to strike 6:00. At lunch it takes more than 12 seconds to strike 12:00. If the clock has not slowed down, how long does it take for the clock to strike? _____

6. Booky, the bookworm, burrowed in a straight line from the first page of Vol. 1 to the last page of Vol. 2 of a collection kept in proper order on a shelf. How far did he burrow if the bindings are ⅛ inch each and the pages are 2½ inch for each book? _____

7. You are trying to walk to school on a very icy sidewalk. The school is 100 yards from your house. For every step you take (1 ft), you slide back 2 ft. You decide it is hopeless, so you turn around to go home. What happens? _____

8. What is the shortest time to grill 3 steaks 20 minutes (10 minutes on a side) if the grill holds two steaks? _____

© Instructional Fair • TS Denison   IF2906 Logic and Critical Thinking

On Second Thought

Name_____

Answer the following questions. Be careful, some of the answers are not what you might think.

1. A part of a wheel is called a *spoke*, a funny story is called a *joke*. What do you call the white of an egg? _____

2. In which direction is Lincoln facing in the famous painting of the "Crossing of the Delaware"? _____

3. What is 200% of 200 divided by 1/2? _____

4. I have 3 coins totaling 25¢. One of the coins is not a nickel. What coins do I have? _____

5. According to the Bible, how many pairs of animals of each kind did Moses take on the ark? _____

6. How much is a $100 suit on sale for 50% off if an additional 20% discount is given? _____

7. How much is 10 thousands + 10 hundreds + 10 ones? _____

8. You have 4 pieces of chain (5 links, 4 links, 3 links, and 2 links). You want a bracelet using all four chains. The jeweler will charge $1.00 to open a link and a $1.25 to weld it closed. What is the least cost? _____

9. If it takes 2 painters 2 hours to paint 2 rooms, how long will it take 4 painters to paint 4 rooms? _____

10. Josh ate all but 2 of a half-dozen cookies. How many cookies were left? _____

11. A pencil costs 15 cents more than an eraser. Jamie paid $.25 for both. How much does an eraser cost? _____

12. Gregory walked 1 mile south, 1 mile east, 1 mile north and was back at his starting point. He saw a bear. What color was the bear? _____

© Instructional Fair • TS Denison   IF2906 *Logic and Critical Thinking*

Name _____

Animal Pathways

Bee Path

Two cyclists start 10 miles apart from each other. One rider travels at 12 miles per hour. The other rides at 8 miles per hour. A bee starts on the shoulder of the first and flies to the shoulder of the second and continues to fly back and forth nonstop until the two cyclists meet. If the bee flies at 15 miles per hour, how far does the bee fly? (Hints: The formula d = rt may be helpful. The bee's rate is 15 mph.) _____

Maze Path

A mouse must walk through the maze below to reach the cheese. The maze measures 40 inches by 40 inches. If the mouse walks down the middle of the path which is 4 inches wide, how far does the mouse walk to reach the cheese? _____

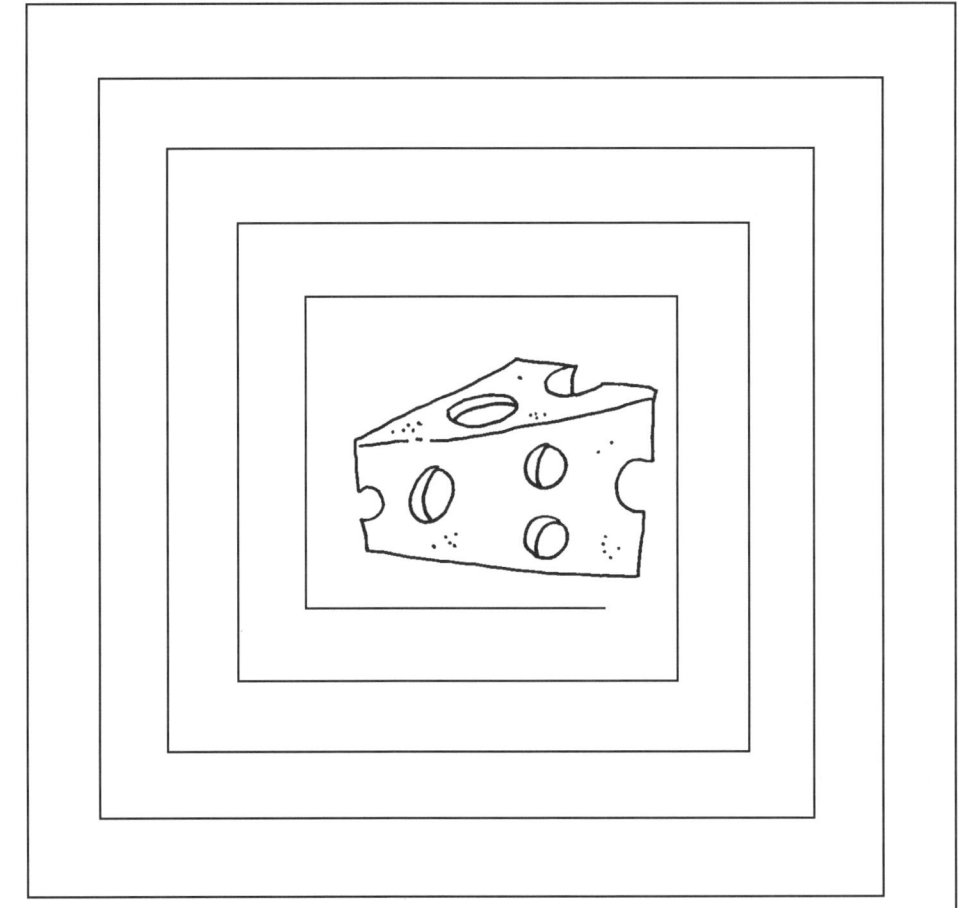

Name_____

WORKING BACKWARDS

Work backwards to solve each problem.

Ups and Downs
Jackie entered the elevator on the floor where her room is located. She went up 3 floors, down 5 floors, and up 10 floors. She got off the elevator to attend a meeting. After the meeting, she rode the elevator down 9 floors, up 4 floors, and finally down 6 floors to the first floor to eat in the restaurant.

On what floor is Jackie's room? _____

Hint: Work backwards from the destination—first floor.

1st floor

Cookie Monster
Cookie Monster opened a box of cookies. He gave half of the cookies to Elmo. Cookie Monster then ate half of the remaining cookies and threw away half a cookie. Grouch came by and Cookie Monster gave him half of the cookies he still had. He again ate half of what was left and threw away half a cookie. Cookie Monster then gave half of the remaining cookies to the Count and ate the last cookie.

How many cookies were in the box? _____

Hint: Work backwards from the last cookie.

Pick a Number
Chris picked a number. He doubled the number then took a third of the result.
After the digits were reversed, Chris added -9, subtracted 8, and divided by -5.
The quotient was -13. What number did Chris pick?

_____

Hint: Work backwards from -13.

© Instructional Fair • TS Denison   25   IF2906 *Logic and Critical Thinking*

BEGIN AT THE END

For each situation, *"begin at the end"* and work backwards.

Prize Money

Alice Benton won a cash prize on a prime-time game show. She celebrated by taking a trip to New York City, which cost her $2,135 and buying a new car, which cost $17,842. Then she donated half of the remaining money to a medical research institution. She bought and sold some profitable stock and made $200 more. After she gave her three sisters $500 each, she had $8,765.

How much was the cash prize? _____

Begin at the end: $8,765

Football Play

Jason's team intercepted the football on their own 21-yard line. Jason made a gain on the first play. Then he was sacked for a 9-yard loss. Jason threw a pass for a 12-yard gain but had a 15-yard penalty. The linebacker then ran for a gain of 27 yards and a first down at the 50-yard line.

How many yards did Jason gain on the first play? _____

Begin at the end:

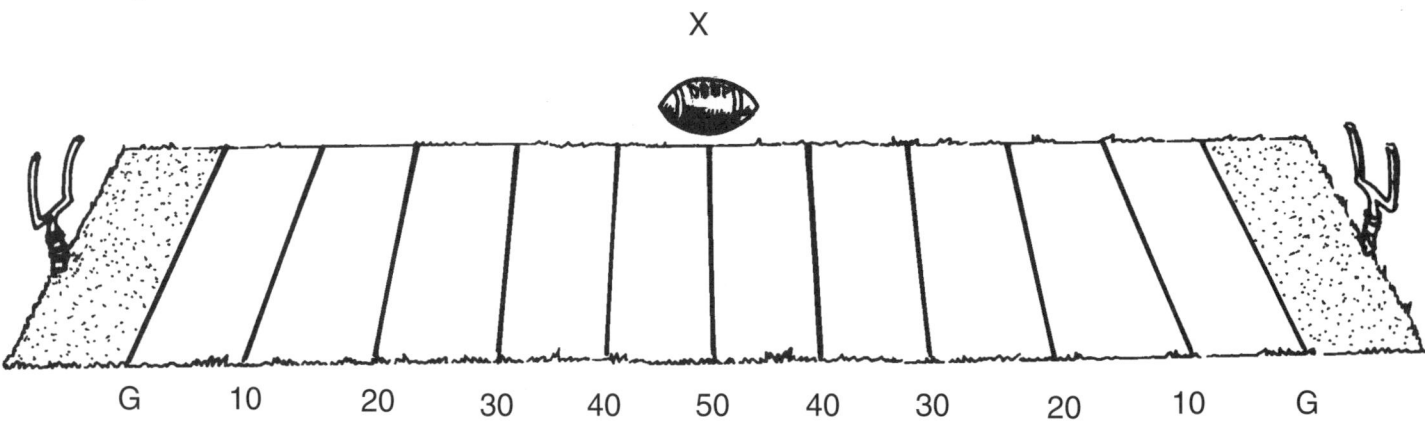

Number Play

Drew picked a number. He multiplied it by 3, subtracted 5, added 11, and divided by 6. After reversing the digits, Drew ended up with 21. What number did Drew pick?

_____

Begin at the end: 21

Name_____

ARROW PATHS

A	B	C	D	E
F	G	H	I	J
K	M	N	O	P
Q	R	S	T	U
V	W	X	Y	Z

Start at the given letter and travel in the direction of the arrows. Find the missing letter.

Example: M → → ↓ ↓ → Z

1. A → → ↓ ↓ ↗ → ↓   __O__

2. E ↓ ↓ ← ← ↑ ↘ ↓   __T__

3. I ← ↑ ← ↓ ↓ → ↓   __S__

4. O ← ↑ ← ↑ → → →   __E__

5. U ↑ ↙ ← ← ↑ ↑ ↘ →   __O__

Start at the given letter and travel in the direction of the arrows. Find the missing arrow.

6. R ↑ → → __↑__ ↓ ↓ T

7. G ↑ ↘ → ↓ ← ↓ __←__ R

8. Z ↖ ← ↑ __→__ → ↓ ↓ Z

9. D ↓ ↓ __↙__ ↓ ← __←__ V

10. H ↑ __→__ ↓ → ↓ __↙__ ↓ Y

Bonus: How is the letter grid related to Christmas? _____

Name_____

NEXT, PLEASE!

Continue each sequence by listing the next three items. Describe the pattern.

1. 1, 1, 2, 3, 5, 8, 13, ____, ____, ____
   _____

2. A, D, G, J, ____, ____, ____
   _____

3. 2, 3, 5, 7, 11, 13, ____, ____, ____
   _____

4. 1, 8, 3, 10, 5, 12, ____, ____, ____
   _____

5. 5, 3, 1, -1, -3, -5, ____, ____, ____
   _____

6. 45°, 90°, 135°, 180°, 225°, ____°, ____°, ____°
   _____

7. II, IV, VI, VIII, X, XII, XIV, XVI, ____, ____, ____
   _____

8. Wyoming, Wisconsin, West Virginia, Washington, Virginia, _____, _____, _____
   _____

9. Triangle, quadrilateral, pentagon, hexagon, _____, _____, _____
   _____

10. Say, you, by, dawn's, light, _____, _____, _____,
    _____

Create a sequence and describe the pattern.
_____
_____

Name _____

PATTERN PROBLEMS

Discover the rule for finding the center number using the four corner numbers. Find the missing center numbers. Describe the rule.

1.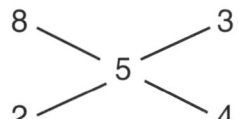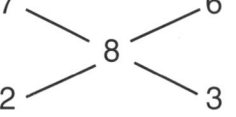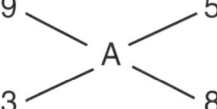

   A = _____ Rule: _____

2.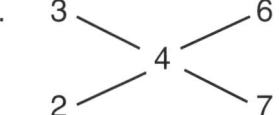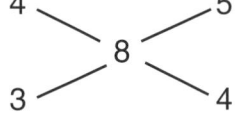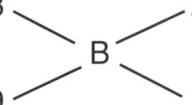

   B = _____ Rule: _____

3.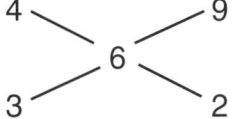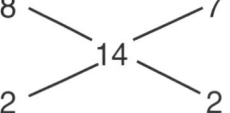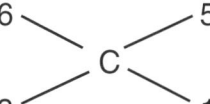

   C = _____ Rule: _____

4.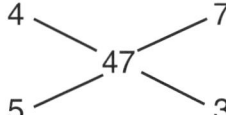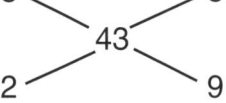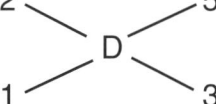

   D = _____ Rule: _____

CHECK: Your answers A, B, C, and D should complete the following:

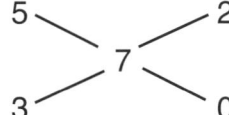 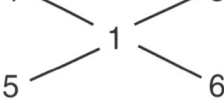 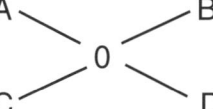

Rule: _____

Code Math

Each digit (0 through 9) has been replaced by a symbol. Use number sense and computation patterns to determine the code. Write the number below its symbol.

★	♥	✳	♣	▲	♦	➩	▶	✓	✗
3	5	1	4	0	6	7	9	8	2

A. ✳ × ★ = ★

B. ✗ + ✗ = ♣

C. ➩ × ✗ = ✳♣

D. ♥ + ♥ = ✳▲

E. ♦ × ♦ = ★♦

F. ✓ + ▶ = ✳➩

G. ✗ × ✗ = ♣

H. ✗♣ ÷ ★ = ✓

Name_____

Gizmos, Whatsits, and Whatchamacallits

1. These are gizmos: These are not gizmos: Which of these are gizmos?

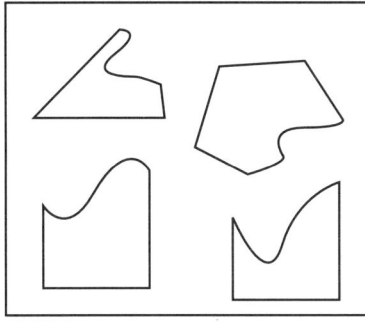  

2. These are whatsits: These are not whatsits: Which of these are whatsits?

A K	B O	F X
H	S	C
E M	P J	D Y Q

3. These are whatchamacallits: These are not whatchamacallits: Which of these are whatchamacallits?

2 11	9 15	17 23
5	8	51
3 7	10 32	6 34 19

4. Make up your own puzzle.
   These are doodads: These are not doodads: Which of these are doodads?

Define a doodad: _____

Name_____

COMMON FEATURES

Determine the number associated with each set of objects. Explain how the number is related to each object.

____ 1. A. ∩ll
      B. dozen
      C. North Carolina
      D. XII
      E. (clock face with arrow pointing up)

A. _____
B. _____
C. _____
D. _____
E. _____

____ 2. A. John Tyler
      B. decade
      C. October
      D. $\sqrt{100}$
      E. decimeter

A. _____
B. _____
C. _____
D. _____
E. _____

____ 3. A. one pound
      B. Tennessee
      C. P
      D. Abraham Lincoln
      E. (4x4 grid)

A. _____
B. _____
C. _____
D. _____
E. _____

____ 4. A. Wyoming
      B. L
      C. Hawaii
      D. half-dollar
      E. half-century

A. _____
B. _____
C. _____
D. _____
E. _____

Name_____

Cube It!

Which of the patterns could be folded into the cube shown? _____

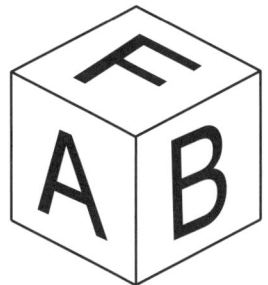      

1.
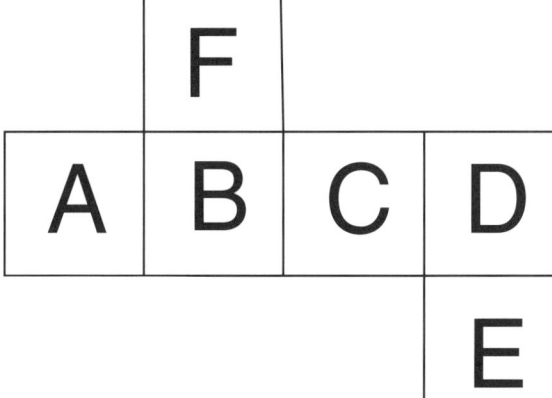

2.
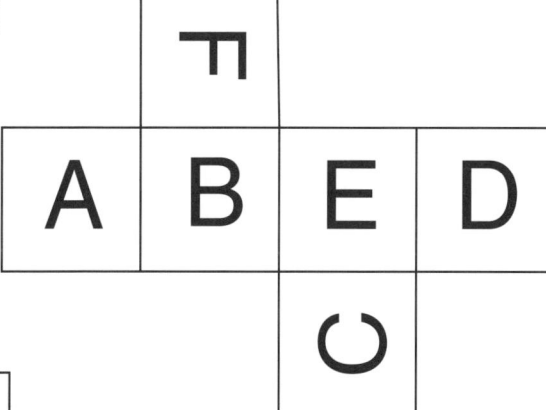

3.

FACE IT!

Name_____

Three views of a cube are given. Label the faces of the cube pattern so if folded it would match the cube.

1.

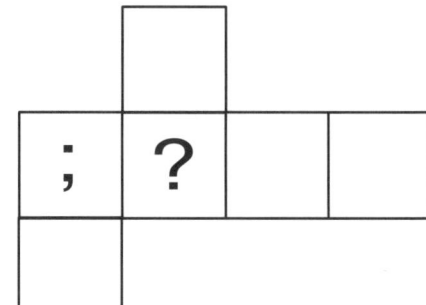

2.

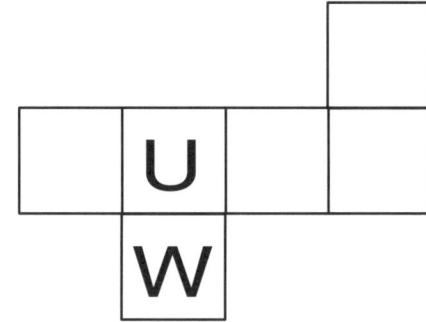

3.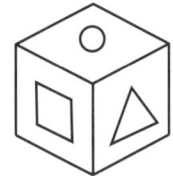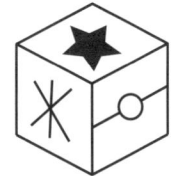

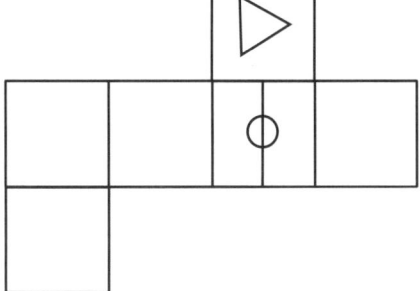

4.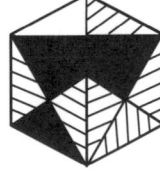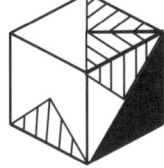

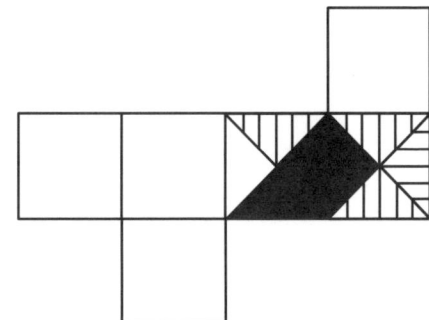

© Instructional Fair • TS Denison   IF2906 *Logic and Critical Thinking*

Name_____

FROM ALL ANGLES

A **base outline** is a top view of a building. A **base plan** is a base outline with numbers indicating the height of each section.

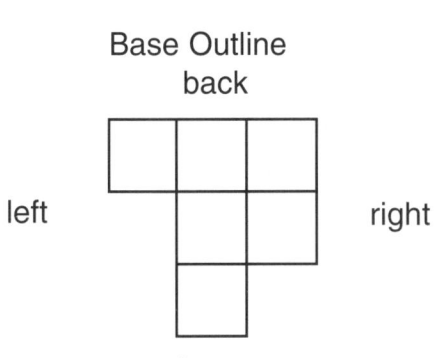

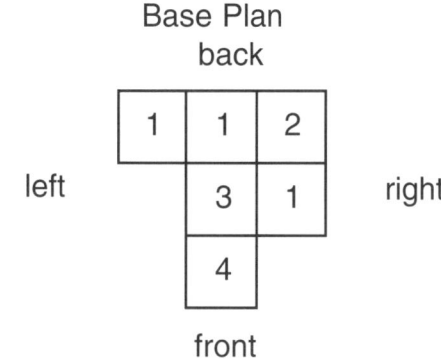

Which side of the building (front, back, left, or right) is represented by each view?

1. 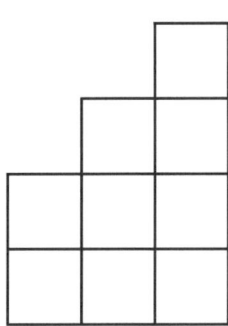 2. 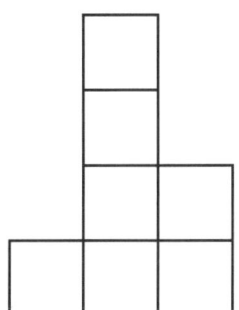 3. 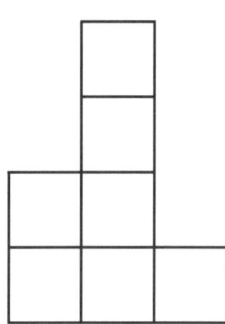 4.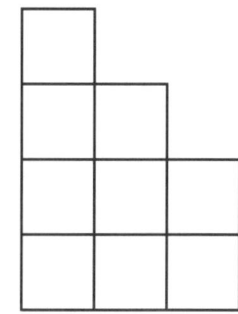

_____ _____ _____ _____

Which corner view (front left, front right, left back, or right back) is shown?

5. 6.

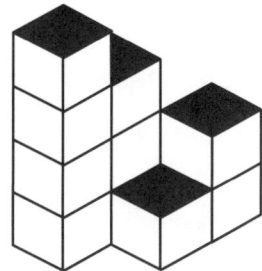   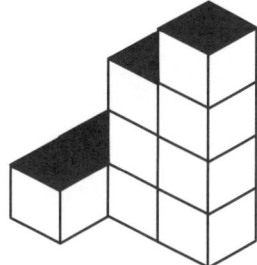

_____   _____

Name _____

COVERING THE BASES

A **base outline** is a top view of a building. A **base plan** is a base outline with numbers indicating the height of each section.

Example:

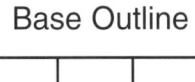
Base Outline
left — front — right

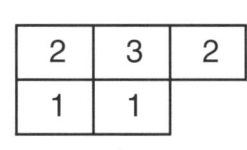
Base Plan
2	3	2
1	1	
left — front — right

1. Label the squares of the base outline to make it a base plan of the building shown.

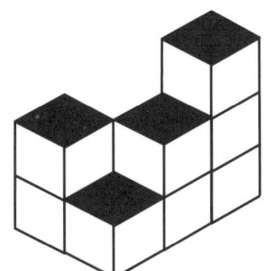

Base Plan
back

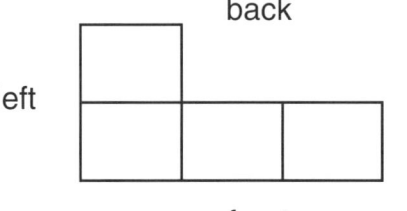

left — front — right

2. Mark with a ✓ the squares of the base plan that could be removed without changing the drawing of the building.

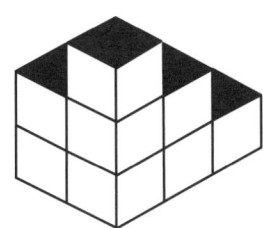

Base Plan
back
2	2	1
3	2	1
left — front — right

3. Complete the drawing of the building represented by the base plan.

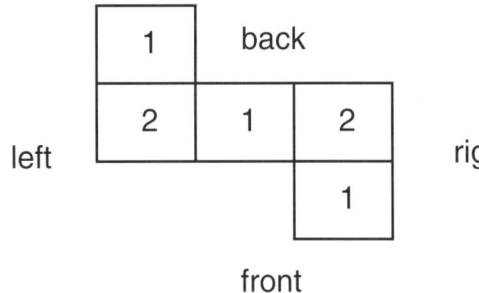

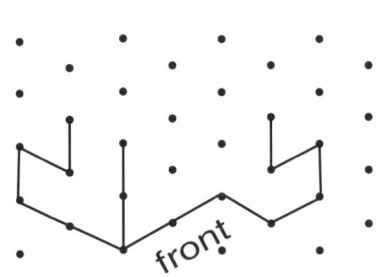

© Instructional Fair • TS Denison   36   IF2906 Logic and Critical Thinking

Name_____

READING REBUSES

A **rebus** is a puzzle consisting of pictures that in combination suggest a word or phrase. Use the clues to solve the following rebuses.

CLUE: Historic figure
1.

_____

CLUE: Literary figure
2.

_____

CLUE: Fictional character
3.

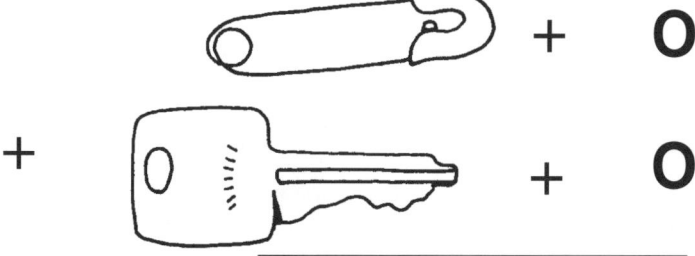

_____

Name_____

READING REBUSES (CONT'D.)

CLUE: Landmark

4. M +  + R

ST + VIII

 + "ding"

_____

CLUE: Inventor

5. RAH +

 +

_____

Create your own rebus.
6.

_____

Name_____

WORD PICTURES

Each pictorial letter arrangement represents a familiar word, name, or phrase. Write your answers on the blanks provided below.

Ex. Number 1 is "head over heels"

1. Head Heels	2. ME (person with long shadow)	3. ROOT	4. POLKA (dotted)
5. FEVER (springs)	6. ALL (stars) GAME	7. Car Car GARAGE	8. 🏠 THE PRAIRIE
9. sleeping THE JOB	10. Niagara (falling)	11. gra AMAZE ce	12. S T O N E
13. H I G H W A Y	14. MAN / BOARD	15. MA ✓ IL	16. for MIS mation

1. _____ 2. _____ 3. _____ 4. _____
5. _____ 6. _____ 7. _____ 8. _____
9. _____ 10. _____ 11. _____ 12. _____
13. _____ 14. _____ 15. _____ 16. _____

Bonus:

Make your own Word Pictures.

© Instructional Fair • TS Denison   39   IF2906 Logic and Critical Thinking

CHEAPER BY THE DOZEN

Rearrange the following squares into the grid below so that the sum of any two adjacent numbers equals 12.

4 **A** 2 3 6	3 **B** 8 9 4	2 **C** 3 1 7
10 **D** 2 5 1	4 **E** 9 11 5	7 **F** 9 1 8
5 **G** 7 4 6	2 **H** 8 9 11	5 **I** 10 11 9

Broken Magic

Name_____

A **Magic Square** is a square arrangement of numbers in which the sum of the numbers in each row, column, and diagonal is the same.

Below are the pieces of a Magic Square. Assemble the pieces into a 4-by-4 Magic Square.

Bingo

Name_____

Assemble the pieces of the Bingo Card in order to complete the Bingo card form.
Note: B's are 1-15, I's are 16-30, N's are 31-45, G's are 46-60, and O's are 61-75.

| 29 | 33 | 48 |

| 9 | 17 | 41 |

| 1 | 18 |
| 2 |
| 5 |

| 70 |
| 75 |
| 66 |

44	47	68
	57
	55

| 10 | 25 |

| 21 | 38 | 50 | 72 |

B	I	N	G	O
		FREE		

© Instructional Fair • TS Denison

Line Up

1. Can you place 8 Xs on the diagram so there are exactly 2 Xs on each straight line and 2 Xs on each circle?

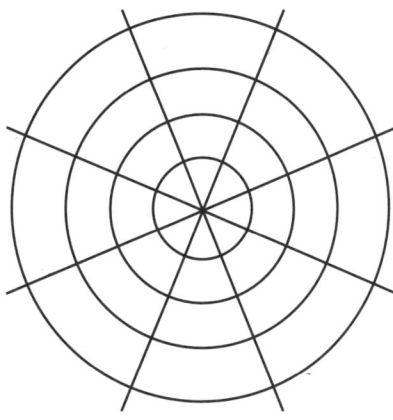

2. Can you place 12 Xs in the 6-by-6 grid so there are no more than 2 Xs in any row, column, or diagonal?

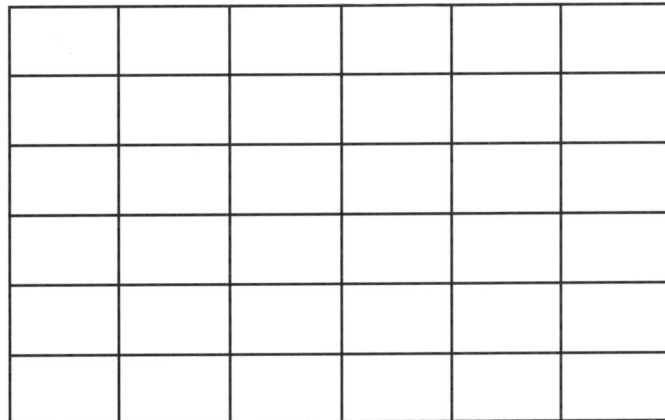

3. Can you place 4 pennies (P), 4 nickels (N), 4 dimes (D), and 4 quarters (Q) in the 4-by-4 grid so no two like coins are in the same row, column, or diagonal?

Digit Math

1. Use the digits 1 through 9 once each to fill in the squares to have a sum of 999.

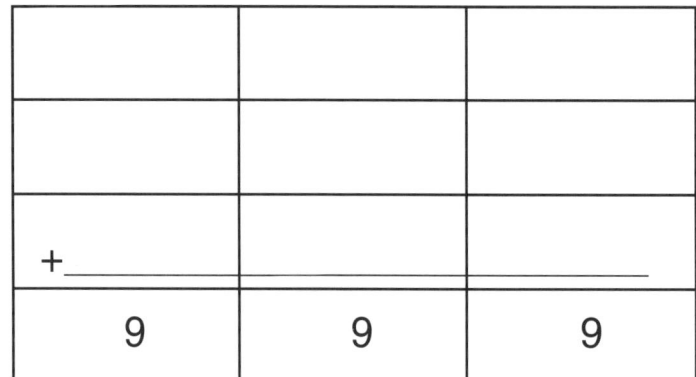

2. Use the digits 1 through 8 once each in the circles so that no two consecutive integers are in circles connected by a line segment.

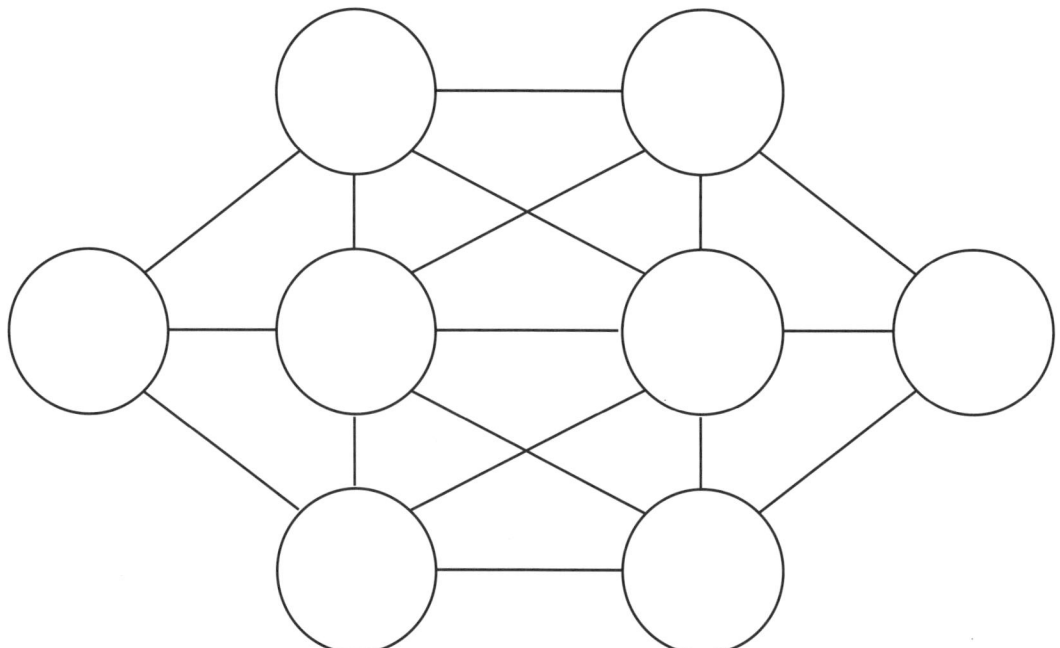

3. Write a 10-digit number in which the first digit tells you the number of zeros there are in the number, the second digit tells how many ones there are in the number, the third digit tells how many twos there are in the number, etc.

___ ___ ___ ___ ___ ___ ___ ___ ___ ___
0s   1s   2s   3s   4s   5s   6s   7s   8s   9s

Answer Key

"X" It Out — page 5
1. Allen lives in Baltimore.
2. Bob lives in Chicago.
3. Carl lives in Erie.
4. David lives in Albany.
5. Earl lives in Denver.

Tea for Two! — page 6
1. Australia 640
2. Great Britain 1355
3. Ireland 1300
4. New Zealand 890
5. Sri Lanka 635
6. Turkey 650

"Climb Every Mountain" — page 7
1. Aconcagua 1897
2. Cook 1894
3. Elbrus 1874
4. Everest 1953
5. Kilimanjaro 1889
6. McKinley 1913
7. Vinson Massif 1966

A Class Act — page 8
1. Ali is enrolled in art and law.
2. Brianna is enrolled in chemistry and engineering.
3. Calli is enrolled in biology and English.

Sports Lunch — page 9
Sam plays hockey.
(Zach plays baseball. Bob plays football. Tony plays basketball.)

Bench Warmers — page 10
1. Steve, Raul, Pat, Tom
2. Dee, Anna, Carol, Betty
   Anna plays violin. Betty plays cello.
3. (Back view) Robert, Bob, Jenny, Margie, Katie
   Jenny sits in the middle.

Table Talk — page 11
1. (circle with numbers 1-14, 12 circled)
2. 22 (10 on each side, 1 at each end)
3. 16 people

4a. 4 tables (8 tables if orientation matters)

4b. 1 x 24; 2 x 12; 3 x 8; 4 x 6
    (24 x 1; 12 x 2; 8 x 3; 6 x 4)

4c. 1 x 24 seats 50; 2 x 12 seats 28; 3 x 8 seats 22;
    4 x 6 seats 20

5. 10 handshakes

How Many Are There? — page 12
1. 12 shirts (blue 4, green 5, striped 1, 2)
2. 8 pets (tail 2, hair 3, 3)
3. 27 students (corn 7, peas 7, beans 2, 5, 3, 3, 3)
4. 25 students (ecology 4, Science Olympiad 12, recycling 3, 3, 3)

Show Me the Graph — page 13
1. F
2. A
3. E
4. B
5. C
6. D

A Graph Is Worth a Thousand Words — page 14
1. A. 1
   B. 6
   C. 3
   D. 2
   E. 4
   F. 5
2. Answers may vary.
   A. Fills the tub with water.
   B. Stops filling tub and gets dog.
   C. Dog is in the tub.
   D. Dog has jumped out of the tub.
   E. Dog is back in the tub (some water is on the floor).
   F. Dog is out of the tub.
   G. Tub is draining (slower rate than the filling).
3. Roller coaster

Balancing Act — page 15
1. □ = ○○
2. △△ = □
3. ○○ = ◯
4. □ = ○○

Pet Shop — page 16
1. Sparrows 12 Spaniels 39
2. Leashes 5 Chew Toys 1
   Seed Packets 94

Get Organized — page 17
1. 2 rectangles: 6 by 3 and 4 by 4
2. 7 benches & 1 stools or
   4 benches & 5 stools or
   1 bench & 9 stools
3. 7 darts-several solutions such as
   5 15s, 1 13, & 1 12
   4 16s & 3 12s
   3 16s & 4 13s
   2 16s & 2 15s & 1 14 & 2 12s
4. 4 single beds and 6 double beds
5. 20 $.33-stamps and 17 $.20-stamps
6. 2 bicycles and 7 tricycles

I Am Unique — page 18
Answers may vary.
2—only even prime
75—only multiple of 15
0.8—only terminating decimal less than 1
12 1/2—only mixed number
1—neither prime nor composite
17—only two-digit prime
-142—only negative integer
√3—only irrational
0.86—only repeating decimal
-1/5—only negative simple fraction
49—only two-digit perfect square
6.7—only mixed decimal number
0—neither positive nor negative
27—only two-digit perfect cube
1,000—only power of ten
2/3—only positive simple fraction
75%—only percent less than 100%
279—only three-digit positive number
3—smallest odd prime
250%—only percent greater than 100%

It's Like — page 19
Answers will vary.
1. Because Jake likes objects with double letters.
2. Because Terry likes spherical objects.
3. Because Sharon likes letters that have vertical-line symmetry. (They can be folded in half lengthwise.)
4. Because Mac likes letters that have horizontal-line symmetry.
5. Because Neil likes odd numbers.
6. Because Nicole likes prime numbers.
7. Because Judy likes odd multiples of 5.

Body Parts — page 20
Some answers may vary.
1. Foot
2. Pupil
3. Eye (Aye, aye)
4. Hand
5. Trunk
6. Teeth
7. Palm
8. Radius
9. Nails
10. Organ
11. Two lips (tulips)
12. Heel
13. Kidney
14. Iris
15. Tongue
16. Sole
17. Hair (hare)
18. Chest
19. Calf
20. Appendix

Initial Equations — page 21
1. Hours in a Day
2. Days in a Year except Leap Year
3. Inches in a Foot
4. Days Hath September, April, June, and November
5. Piano Keys
6. Cents in a Dollar
7. Planets in the Solar System
8. Letters of the Alphabet
9. Degrees in a Right Angle
10. Quarts in a Gallon
11. Stripes on the American Flag
12. Ounces in a Pound
13. Meters in a Kilometer
14. Innings in a Baseball Game
15. Degrees Celsius at which Water Freezes
16. Months in a Year
17. Cards in a Deck
18. Seconds in a Minute
19. Pounds in a Ton
20. Degrees in a Circle

Everyone's a Critic — page 22
1. 29 days—It would double to cover the pond on day 30.
2. The first trucker took longer. First trucker: 150mi/50mph + 150mi/60mph = 5 1/2 (Cannot average the rates because the times are different.)
   Second trucker: 300 mi/55 mph = 5 5/11 h
3. About 3 inches. The needle does not travel "around the record." The record spins "under the needle."
4. It cannot be done. One lap at 30 mph takes 2 minutes. To average 60 mph for two laps, the driver needs to travel the two laps in 2 minutes. He would have to travel the second lap in zero time.
5. 6 sec/5 = 1 1/5 sec. When a clock strikes 12:00 there are 11 "time slots" compared to 5 "time slots for 6:00 so the time would be more than double—13 1/5 sec
6. 1/4 inch. The front cover of Vol. 1 would be next to the back cover of Vol. 2 so Booky only burrowed through the two bindings (1/8 + 1/8)
7. As you try to walk home, you will actually move a step toward the school. 300 steps later you will be at the school.
8. 30 minutes. Number the steaks 1, 2, and 3 and the two sides as A and B. Grill 1A and 2A for 10 minutes. Grill 1B with 3A for 10 minutes. Grill 2B with 3B for 10 minutes.

On Second Thought — page 23
1. Albumen. The yolk is the yellow part.
2. Lincoln is not in the painting. It is George Washington.
3. 800—200% x 200 ÷ 1/2 = 2 x 200 x 2
4. 2 dimes and 1 nickel (One of the coins is not a nickel, but another coin could be.)
5. It was Noah, not Moses.
6. $40 not $30
7. 11,010
8. $6.75—Open and weld closed 3 links. Open the 3 links of the 3-link chain and use them to join the other 3 pieces into a single chain.
9. 2 hours. 1 painter could paint 1 room in 2 hours, so 4 painters could paint 4 rooms in the same time.
10. 2 not 4
11. $.05—The pencil would cost $.20.
12. White. He is at the North Pole.

Animal Pathways — page 24
Bee Path—7½ miles
The two cyclists will meet in 1/2 hour. If the bee flies nonstop for 1/2 hour, it will fly 7 1/2 miles.
Maze Path—400 in.
The maze has an area of 1600 sq. in. "Unwrap" the maze into a long rectangle. The width is 4 in. So the length would be 400 inches—1600/4.

Working Backwards — page 25
1. 4th floor
   Working backwards: 1 + 6 - 4 + 9 - 10 + 5 - 3 = 4

2. 42 cookies
   Working backwards: (1 last cookie + 1 given to the Count + 1/2 thrown away) x 2 before Grouch = 5; (5 + 5 given to Grouch + 1/2 thrown away) x 2 before Elmo = 21; (21 + 21 given to Elmo) = 42
3. 42
   Working backwards:
   13 x -5 + 8 - (-9) = 82 → 28 x 3 ÷ 2 = 42

Begin at the End   page 26
Prize Money—$40,107
(8,765 + 3 x 500 - 200) x 2 + 17,842 + 2,135
Football Play—14 yards
50 - 27 + 15 - 12 + 9 = 35 - 21 = 14-yard play
Number Play—22
21 → 12 x 6 -11 + 5 = 66; 66/3 = 22

Arrow Paths   page 27
1. P
2. T
3. S
4. E
5. O
6. ↑
7. ←
8. →
9. ← ↙ one possibility
10. ↙ → one possibility

Bonus: Noel (No L)

Next, Please!   page 28
1. 21, 34, 55—Add the two preceding numbers.
2. M, P, S—Skip two letters
3. 17, 19, 23—Prime numbers
4. 7, 14, 9—Add 7 subtract 5
5. -7, -9, -11—Subtract 2
6. 270°, 315°, 360°—Adding 45°
7. XVIII, XX, XXII—Adding 2 in Roman numerals
8. Vermont, Utah, Texas—states in reverse alphabetical order
9. Heptagon, Octagon, Nonagon—names of polygons adding 1 to the number of sides
10. So, we, at—alternate words of "The Star-Spangled Banner"

Pattern Problems   page 29
A = 3 (sum of top 2 #s) - (sum of bottom 2 #s)
B = 7 (product of top 2 #s) - (product of bottom 2#s)
C = 10 (product of top 2 #s) ÷ (product of bottom 2 #s)
D = 11 Sum of the products of diagonal numbers
Check: (product of top 2#s) - (sum of bottom 2#s)

Code Math   page 30

★	♥	✳	♣	▲	♦	⇨	▶	✓	✗
3	5	1	4	0	6	7	9	8	2

Gizmos, Whatsits, and Whatchamacallits   page 31
1. 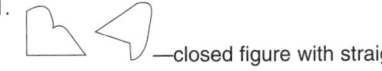—closed figure with straight and curved sides
2. F, X, Y—made with straight lines
3. 17, 19, 23—prime numbers

Common Features   page 32
1. 12
   A. 12 in Egyptian Numerals
   B. Equals 12 objects
   C. 12th colony to become a state
   D. 12 in Roman Numerals
   E. Clock at 12:00
2. 10
   A. Tenth president
   B. Equals 10 years
   C. Tenth month
   D. Square root of 100 = 10
   E. 10 decimeters = meter
3. 16
   A. 16 ounces
   B. Sixteenth state admitted to the Union
   C. Sixteenth letter of the alphabet
   D. Sixteenth president
   E. Area = 16
4. 50
   A. Fiftieth state in alphabetical order
   B. 50 in Roman numerals
   C. Fiftieth state admitted to the Union
   D. 50 cents
   E. 1/2 x 100 years = 50 years

Cube It!   page 33
Cube 3

Face It!   page 34
1.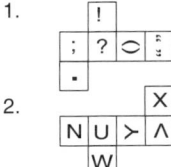
2.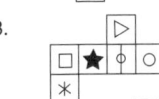
3.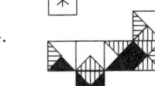
4.

From All Angles   page 35
1. Left
2. Front
3. Back
4. Right
5. Front right
6. Front left

Covering the Bases   page 36
1.
2.
3.

Reading Rebuses   page 37
1. Winston Churchill
2. Lady Macbeth
3. Pinocchio

Reading Rebuses (cont.)   page 38
4. Empire State Building
5. Robert Fulton

Word Pictures   page 39
1. Head over heels
2. Me and my shadow
3. Square root
4. Polka dots
5. Spring fever
6. All-star game
7. Two-car garage
8. *Little House on the Prairie*
9. Sleeping on the job
10. Niagara Falls
11. Amazing Grace
12. Cornerstone
13. Divided highway
14. Man overboard
15. Check is in the mail
16. Misinformation

Cheaper by the Dozen   page 40
One possibility:

G	I	C
H	A	D
F	B	E

Broken Magic page 41

25	1	12	7
11	8	24	2
5	10	3	27
4	26	6	9

BINGO page 42

B	I	N	G	O
10	25	44	47	68
9	17	41	57	70
1	18	FREE	55	75
2	29	33	48	66
5	21	38	50	72

Line Up page 43
Other answers are possible.
1.

2.

x		x		
x		x		
	x		x	
	x		x	
		x		x
	x		x	

3. One possible answer:

P	N	D	Q
Q	D	N	P
N	P	Q	D
D	Q	P	N

Digit Math page 44
1. 359
    468
    <u>172</u>
    999

2.

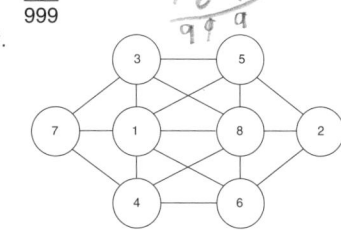

3. 6210001000